Star

my guide to the solar system

CHERRY LAKE PRESS

Published in the United States of America by Cherry Lake Publishing
Ann Arbor, Michigan
www.cherrylakepublishing.com

Reading Adviser: Beth Walker Gambro, MS, Ed., Reading Consultant, Yorkville, IL
Book Design: Jennifer Wahi
Illustrator: Jeff Bane

Photo Credits: © Nikolay Pandev/iStock.com, 5; © pixelparticle/iStock.com, 7; © Jurik Peter/Shutterstock.com, 9; © Art-Perfect/Shutterstock.com, 11; © Alexxandar/Shutterstock.com, 13; © Denis Belitsky/Shutterstock.com, 15; © Paul Orr/Shutterstock.com, 17; © MoVille/Shutterstock.com, 19; © NASA images/Shutterstock.com, 21; © songqiuju/iStock.com, 23; Cover, 2-3, 8, 10, 22, 24, Jeff Bane

Copyright © 2022 by Cherry Lake Publishing Group
All rights reserved. No part of this book may be reproduced or utilized in any form or by any means without written permission from the publisher.

Cherry Lake Press is an imprint of Cherry Lake Publishing Group.

Library of Congress Cataloging-in-Publication Data

Names: Devera, Czeena, author. | Bane, Jeff, 1957- illustrator.
Title: Star / by Czeena Devera ; illustrated by Jeff Bane.
Description: Ann Arbor, Michigan : Cherry Lake Publishing, [2022] | Series: My guide to the solar system | Audience: Grades K-1
Identifiers: LCCN 2021036768 (print) | LCCN 2021036769 (ebook) | ISBN 9781534199026 (hardcover) | ISBN 9781668890161 (paperback) | ISBN 9781668905920 (ebook) | ISBN 9781668901601 (pdf)
Subjects: LCSH: Stars--Juvenile literature.
Classification: LCC QB801.7 .D48 2023 (print) | LCC QB801.7 (ebook) | DDC 523.8--dc23
LC record available at https://lccn.loc.gov/2021036768
LC ebook record available at https://lccn.loc.gov/2021036769

Printed in the United States of America
Corporate Graphics

glossary & index

glossary

dense (DENS) having parts that are very close together

dwarfs (DWORFs) smaller stars, like Earth's Sun

gravity (GRAH-vuh-tee) a force that attracts and pulls down objects

nebula (NEH-byuh-luh) a cloud of gas and dust in space

neutrons (NOO-trons) stars formed from dying stars

scientists (SYE-uhn-tists) people who study nature and the world we live in

sequence (SEE-kwuhns) a group of things that come one after another

solar system (SOH-luhr SIH-stuhm) a star and the planets that move around it

supernova (soo-puhr-NOH-vuh) the explosion of a star

index

dwarfs, 14, 16

giants, 14, 18
gravity, 8

neutrons, 14, 20

red giant, 10

solar system, 18
space, 4

Scientists are still studying me. There's so much more to learn!

Neutron stars are tiny and very **dense**. They form from stars that have exploded.

Giant stars are exactly that—giant! They look blue. They are really bright. Some stars are supergiants. They can be as big as a **solar system**!

17

Dwarf stars are small to medium in size. The Sun is actually a dwarf star!

We can be one of many types. The main types are **dwarfs**, giants, and **neutrons**.

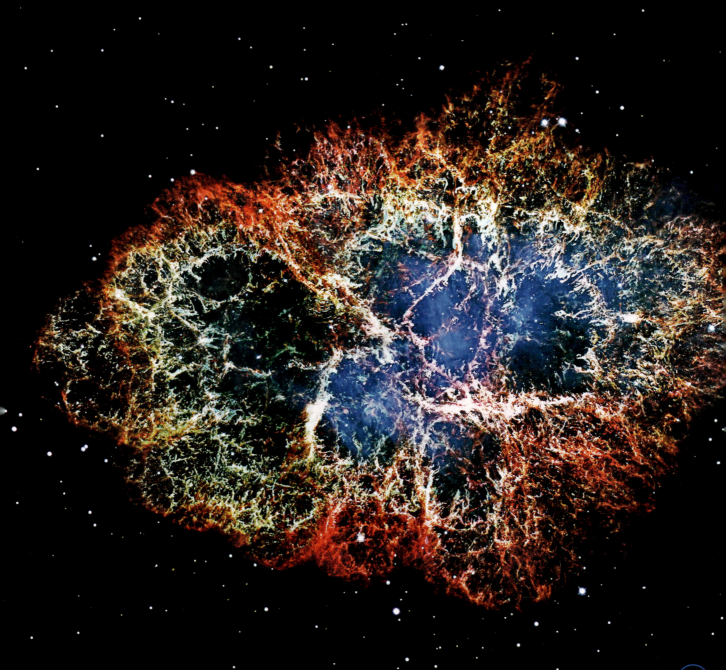

Eventually, I explode and become a **supernova**. Then the cycle begins again.

I glow for billions of years. This part of my life is called the main **sequence**. Then I become a red giant.

Gravity forces this giant cloud to come together. I become really hot. I finally form into a young star.

I start out as a giant cloud of dust and gas. This is called a **nebula**. The cloud usually comes from a dying star.

5

Star

I'm a star. I live in outer space.

table of contents

Star 4

Glossary 24

Index 24

About the author: Czeena Devera grew up in the red-hot heat of Arizona surrounded by books. Her childhood bedroom had built-in bookshelves that were always full. She now lives in Michigan with an even bigger library of books.

About the illustrator: Jeff Bane and his two business partners own a studio along the American River in Folsom, California, home of the 1849 Gold Rush. When Jeff's not sketching or illustrating for clients, he's either swimming or kayaking in the river to relax.